This book belongs to

_____

*This book is dedicated to the fierce Claire Huxtable,
the boss Maxine Shaw, and the stylish Joan Clayton
for showing me and other young Black girls
that we could be lawyers.
May this book serve as the vision and inspiration
for other young Black children, and children
generally, as these fictional TV lawyers did for me.*

Designed and illustrated by Ira Baykovska

ISBN: 978-1-7355225-7-9

LCCN: 2021919256

Andrew Learns about Lawyers

part of Andrew's
"Career Day" Book Series

Tiffany Obeng

On the fourth Thursday in April,
Andrew woke when his clock alarmed.
He threw back the covers, leapt from bed
and ran straight into Mama's arms.

Today was "Take your child to work day"
and Andrew could not wait!
He was going to work with Mama.
He knew it would be great!

But then Andrew hung his head
and Mama asked,
"Hey, what's wrong with you?"
Andrew said, "It just occurred to me
that I don't know what you do?"

Mama chuckled, "Oh that's all."
And she said "Well, that's easy."
Then she said, "I am a lawyer,
also known as an attorney (uh-turn-nee)."

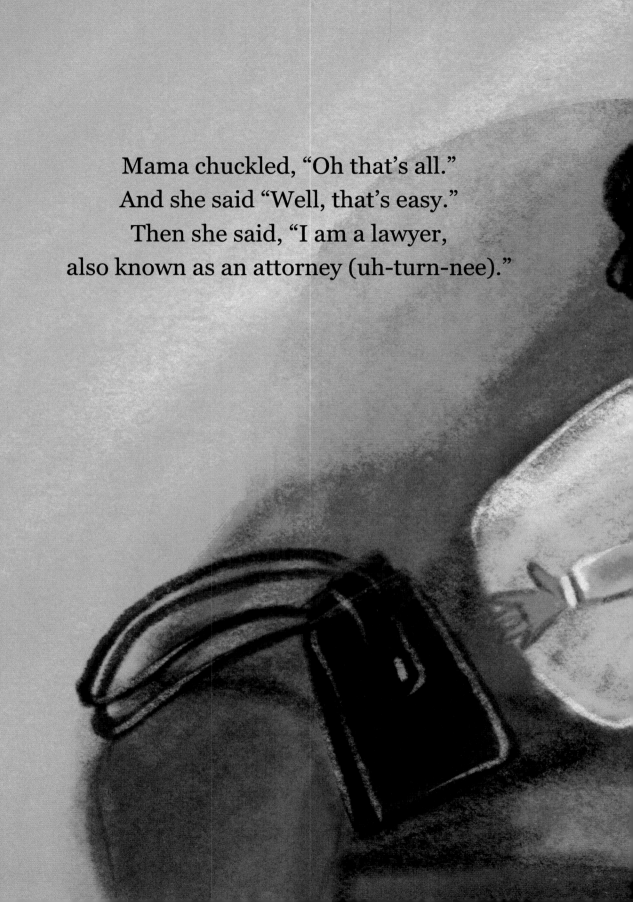

You know how we always stop
our car at a red traffic light?
Or how we know that taking from others
is something that's not right?

Well, we know this because they are laws,
and they tell us what to do.

You can think of laws as
society's (so-sy-e-tee)
set of rules.

And you know how I explain to you
the rules of a new game?
Lawyers explain the laws to people.
It's a little bit the same.

Lawyers listen to people's problems
and they come up with a plan.
Lawyers help people protect their rights.
Lawyers help people take a stand!

Lawyers think, they read, they argue.
They also write a lot.
Lawyers problem solve, may go to court,
they give it all they've got!

And, there's so many types of lawyers.
Not all lawyers are the same.
I'll tell you of a few different lawyers
and their specific aim.

A family lawyer helps us with issues involving kids, moms and dads.

FAMILY LAW

And a criminal lawyer helps those accused of doing something bad.

A business lawyer helps people start
and run their company.

An immigration
(m-ma-gray-shun)
lawyer helps visitors
stay in our country.

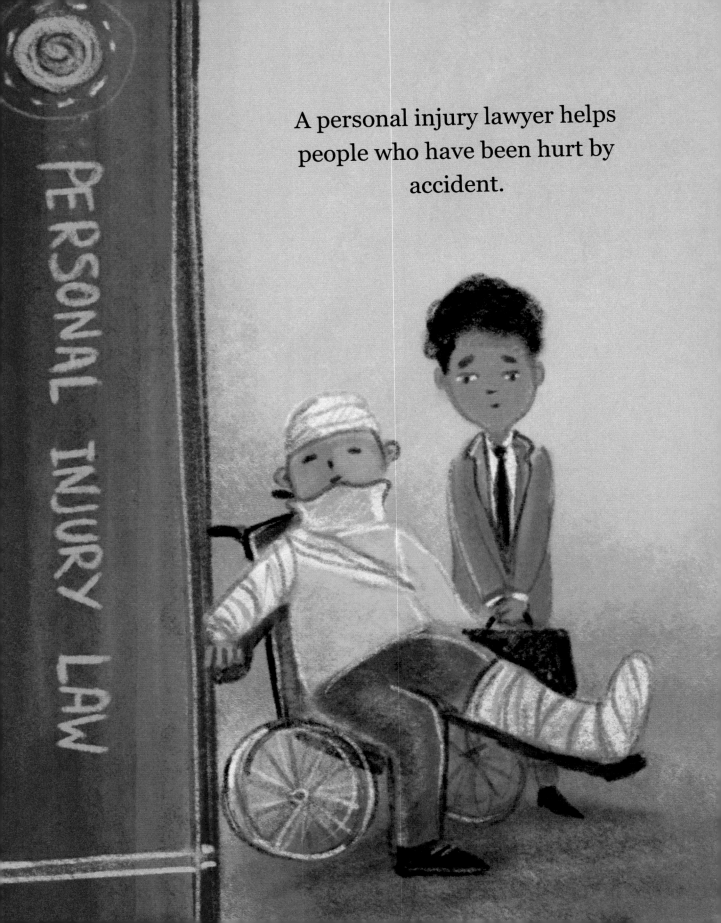

A personal injury lawyer helps people who have been hurt by accident.

And bankruptcy (bank-rup-see) lawyers help us out of trouble when all our money is spent.

Some lawyers become **judges, mayors, governors** or **presidents.**
And some lawyers become **statesmen** or **civil rights activists** (ak-tuh-vist).

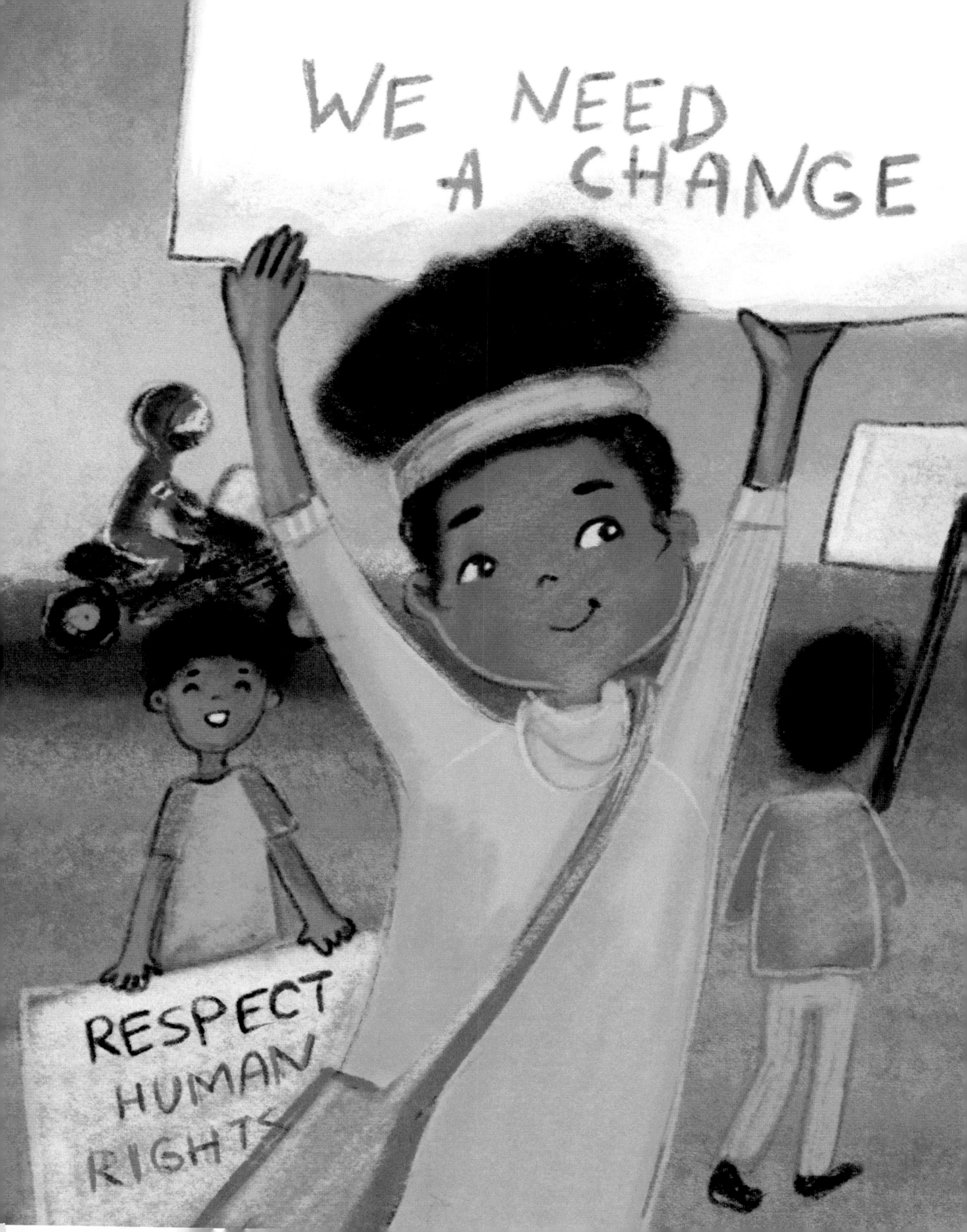
WE NEED A CHANGE
RESPECT HUMAN RIGHTS

Being a lawyer is hard work,
but it's also rewarding.
It feels great to be a part of change
or even history.

Like,
Thurgood Marshall,
Ruth Bader Ginsburg,
Barbara Jordan
and **Fred Gray.**
These are a few groundbreaking
lawyers who all helped pave the way.

We could go on and on,
but that's all for now, you see.
We must get going to work, so let's
get ready, let's hurry.

"Could I be a lawyer, too?"
Andrew turned and asked Daddy.
Daddy said, **"Of course, you can.
You can be anything you want to be!"**

Glossary:

Barbara Jordan: Black female lawyer, educator and politician

Civil rights activist: people who fight for the rights of all people

Fred Gray: Black male lawyer, preacher and activist

Governor: a person selected to be in charge of the state

Judge: a person who is in charge of court

Mayor: a person selected to be in charge of the city or town

President: a person selected to be in charge of the country

Ruth Bader Ginsburg: White female lawyer and second female judge on the U.S. Supreme Court

Statesmen: an important, well-known person who creates laws

Thurgood Marshall: Black male lawyer and first Black judge on the U.S. Supreme Court

With your parents' permission and help, search on your computer or go to your local library or bookstore to learn more about Barbara Jordan, Fred Gray, Ruth Bader Ginsburg and Thurgood Marshall!

Hi readers!

Thanks for reading *Andrew Learns about Lawyers*. As a lawyer myself, the book was a true labor of love. I enjoyed being able to teach my little one about my career as a lawyer and I hope you enjoyed learning about lawyers!

As a lawyer and children's book author, it is important to me to write fun rhyming books that introduce young kids to possible careers and empower their present and their future. My goal is to help children decide their futures, one book at a time! Check out other books in the series and by me at www.SugarCookieBooks.com.

Tiffany Obeng

SugarCookieBooks@gmail.com
@SugarCookieBooks

If you liked this book, please leave an honest
5-star review on Amazon.com!

Other books by Tiffany Obeng:
Andrew Learns about Actors (2020)
Andrew Learns about Teachers (2021)
Scout's Honor: A Kid's Book about Lying and Telling the Truth (2021)
Winnie Loves Winter: A Book about the Winter Season (2021)

65358179R10026